Great
Start!

**Purchased with
Smart Start Funds**

To parents and teachers

We hope you and the children will enjoy reading this story in either English or Spanish. The story is simple, but not *simplified,* so the language of the Spanish and the English is quite natural but there is lots of repetition.

At the back of the book is a small picture dictionary with the key words and how to pronounce them. There is also a simple pronunciation guide to the whole story on the last page.

Here are a few suggestions on using the book:

- Read the story aloud in English first, to get to know it. Treat it like any other picture book: look at the pictures, talk about the story and the characters and so on.

- Then look at the picture dictionary and say the Spanish names for the key words. Ask the children to repeat them. Concentrate on speaking the words out loud, rather than reading them.

- Go back and read the story again, this time in English *and* Spanish. Don't worry if your pronunciation isn't quite correct. Just have fun trying it out. Check the guide at the back of the book, if necessary, but you'll soon pick up how to say the Spanish words.

- When you think you and the children are ready, you can try reading the story in Spanish only. Ask the children to say it with you. Only ask them to read it if they are eager to try. The spelling could be confusing and put them off.

- Above all encourage the children to have a go and give lots of praise. Little children are usually quite unselfconscious and this is excellent for building up confidence in a foreign language.

First edition for the United States and Canada published 1994 by Barron's Educational Series, Inc.
Text © Copyright 1994 by b small publishing, Surrey, England
Illustrations © Copyright 1994 by Steve Weatherill
Address all inquiries to: Barron's Educational Series, Inc., 250 Wireless Boulevard, Hauppauge, New York 11788
International Standard Book Number 0-8120-6451-8   Library of Congress Catalog Card Number 94-563
Printed in Hong Kong   567   9598   9876

I'm too big

Soy demasiado grande

Lone Morton

From an idea by Ella McCourt

Pictures by Steve Weatherill
Spanish by Rosa Martín

I'm too big.

Yo soy demasiado grande.

I'm too tall.

Yo soy demasiado alta.

I want a long neck.

Yo quiero un cuello largo.

I want big ears.

Yo quiero unas orejas grandes.

I don't like my long nose!
I want a short one.

¡No me gusta mi nariz larga!
Quiero una corta.

I don't like my long neck!
I want a short one.

¡No me gusta mi cuello largo!
Quiero uno corto.

I don't like grey.
I want to be yellow like you.

No me gusta el gris.
Quiero ser amarillo como tú.

I like grey.
I want to be grey like you.

Me gusta el gris.
Quiero ser gris como tú.

But I want shorter legs …

Pero quiero patas más cortas …

... and a bigger head.

... y una cabeza más grande.

I want a longer tail ...

Quiero una cola más larga ...

... and a smaller head.

... y una cabeza más pequeña.

Yes, I want a longer tail ...

Sí, yo quiero una cola más larga...

... and a longer nose.

... y una nariz más larga.

But wait!
I like you as you are.

¡Pero, oye!
Me gustas tal como eres.

And you're fine as you are.

Y tú también, estás bien así.

Yes ... we're great like this!

¡Sí ... estamos muy bien así!

Pronouncing Spanish

Don't worry if your pronunciation isn't quite correct. The important thing is to be willing to try.

The pronunciation guide is based on the Spanish accent used in Latin America. Although it cannot be completely accurate, it certainly will be a great help.

• Read the guide as naturally as possible, as if it were English.

• Put stress on the letters in *italics,* e.g., *kwel*-yo.

If you can, ask a Spanish-speaking person to help and move on as soon as possible to speaking the words without the guide.

Note: Spanish adjectives usually have two forms, one for masculine and one for feminine nouns. They often look very similar but are pronounced slightly differently, e.g., **largo** and **larga** (see on the right).

Words Las palabras

lass pal-*abrass*

grey

gris

greess

yellow

amarillo/amarilla

amma-*ree*-yo/amma-*ree*-ya

big
grande
grandeh

tall
alto/alta
alto/alta

small
pequeño/pequeña
pek*ken*-yo/pek*ken*-ya

short
corto/corta
corto/corta

long
largo/larga
largo/larga

head
la cabeza
lah *cabesa*

ear
la oreja
lah or*ray*-ha

nose
la nariz
lah na*rees*

neck
el cuello
el *kwel*-yo

tail
la cola
lah *cola*

leg
la pata
lah *patta*

A simple guide to pronouncing this Spanish story

Soy demasiado grande.
soy demass-*yaddo* *grandeh*

Yo soy demasiado alta.
yo soy demass-*yaddo* *al*ta

Yo quiero un cuello largo.
yo kee-*yerro* oon *kwel*-yo *largo*

Yo quiero unas orejas grandes.
yo kee-*yerro* *oon*as or*ray*-hass *grandes*

¡No me gusta mi nariz larga!
noh meh *goos*ta mee na*rees* *lar*ga

Quiero una corta.
kee-*yerro* *oon*a *corta*

¡No me gusta mi cuello largo!
noh meh *goos*ta mee *kwel*-yo *lar*go

Quiero uno corto.
kee-*yerro* *oon*o *corto*

No me gusta el gris.
noh meh *goos*ta el greess

Quiero ser amarillo como tú.
kee-*yerro* sair amma-*ree*-yo *commo* too

Me gusta el gris.
meh *goos*ta el greess

Quiero ser gris como tú.
kee-*yerro* sair greess *commo* too

Pero quiero patas más cortas ...
perro kee-*yerro* *pat*tas mass *cor*tas

y una cabeza más grande.
ee *oon*a ca*bes*a mass *grandeh*

Quiero una cola más larga ...
kee-*yerro* *oon*a *co*lla mass *lar*ga

y una cabeza más pequeña.
ee *oon*a ca*bes*a mass pek*ken*-ya

Sí, yo quiero una cola más larga ...
see yo kee-*yerro* *oon*a *co*lla mass *lar*ga

y una nariz más larga.
ee *oon*a na*rees* mass *lar*ga

¡Pero, oye!
perro *oy*eh!

Me gustas tal como eres.
meh *goos*tass tahl *commo* *ehrehs*

Y tú también estás bien así.
ee too tamb-*yen* es*tass* b-*yen* as*see*

¡Sí ... estamos muy bien así!
see ... es*tam*mos mwee b-*yen* as*see*!